The Technique of the Flute

CHORD STUDIES

JOSEPH VIOLA

Berklee Press
Publications

EXCLUSIVELY DISTRIBUTED BY

HAL•LEONARD®
CORPORATION

7777 W. BLUEMOUND RD. P.O. BOX 13819 MILWAUKEE, WI 53213

AUTHOR'S NOTES

To derive the most benefit from the exercises in this book it is important that the following practice procedure be followed with each new chord covered in Section I.

A. Preparatory Exercises

(1) Play the basic chord (1, 3, 5, or 1, 3, 5, 7) several times until the tonality is firmly fixed in your ear.

(2) Add high degrees one at a time.   Try to hear the relationship of each tension to the basic chord.

(3) Where altered tensions are indicated, relate each altered form to the basic chord.

B.   Exercises employing chord tones and auxiliary tones. (Exercises 1, 2 and 3 of each chord.)

(1) Listen for the resolution of each auxiliary tone as it moves into the basic chord tone.

(2) After repeating each exercise several times, play it without looking at the music.   Concentrate on remembering the chord tones and let your ear assist you in finding the proper auxiliary tones.

C.   Exercises employing low degree chord tones, high degree chord tones and auxiliary tones. (Exercises 4 and 5 of each chord.)

(1) Be aware of the tonality of the basic chord at all times. If the tonality seems vague, stop and play the basic chord several times before repeating the exercise.

(2) Experiment with various articulations.   Suggested variations are
    indicated below.

Even where not theoretically required, accidentals have been repeated
to assure an awareness of the proper note.

All of the exercises may (and should) be played at different tempos and
with variations in phrasing and interpretation.

The augmented chord has not been included since it is considered to be
an altered form of the dominant seventh.

                                                    J.V.

Table of Contents

SECTION I

Studies on Chord Structures

C major

C minor

C seventh

C minor seventh

Cm7

Cm7

C minor seventh (flat five)

Cm7(b5)

C diminished seventh

1

2

3

4
C°7

5
C°7

F major

F minor

12

Fm

Fm

Fm

Fm

13

F seventh

F minor seventh

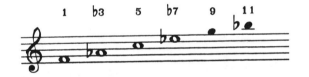

16

F minor seventh (flat five)

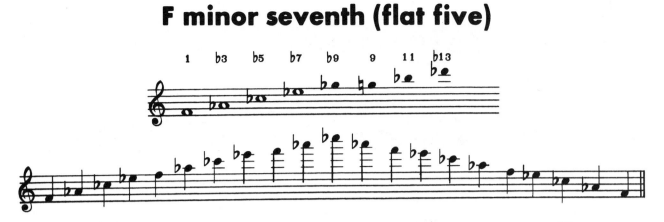

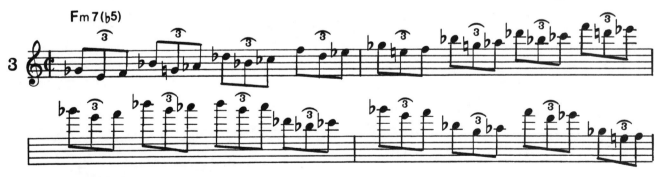

17

F diminished seventh

2

3

4

5

G major

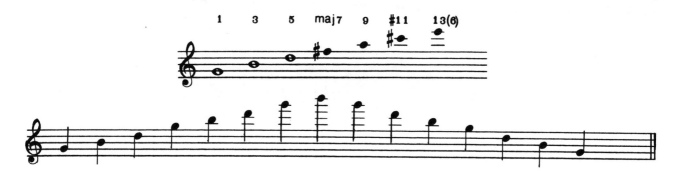

G minor

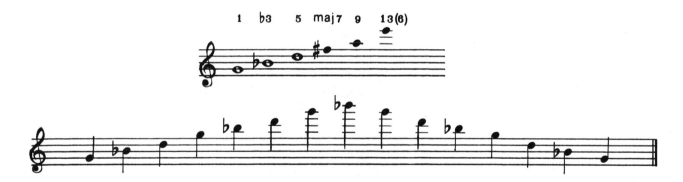

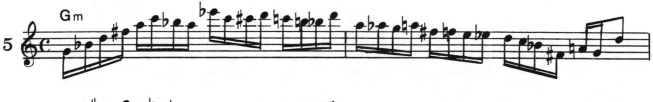

G seventh

1

2

3

4

5

G minor seventh

1

G minor seventh (flat five)

26

4 Gm7(b5)

5 Gm7(b5)

G diminished seventh

1 G°7

G°7

2

3

4

5

B♭ major

B♭ minor

B♭ seventh

32

Bb7

Bb7

Bb minor seventh

Bbm7

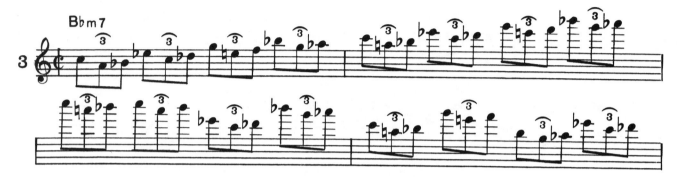

B♭ minor seventh (flat five)

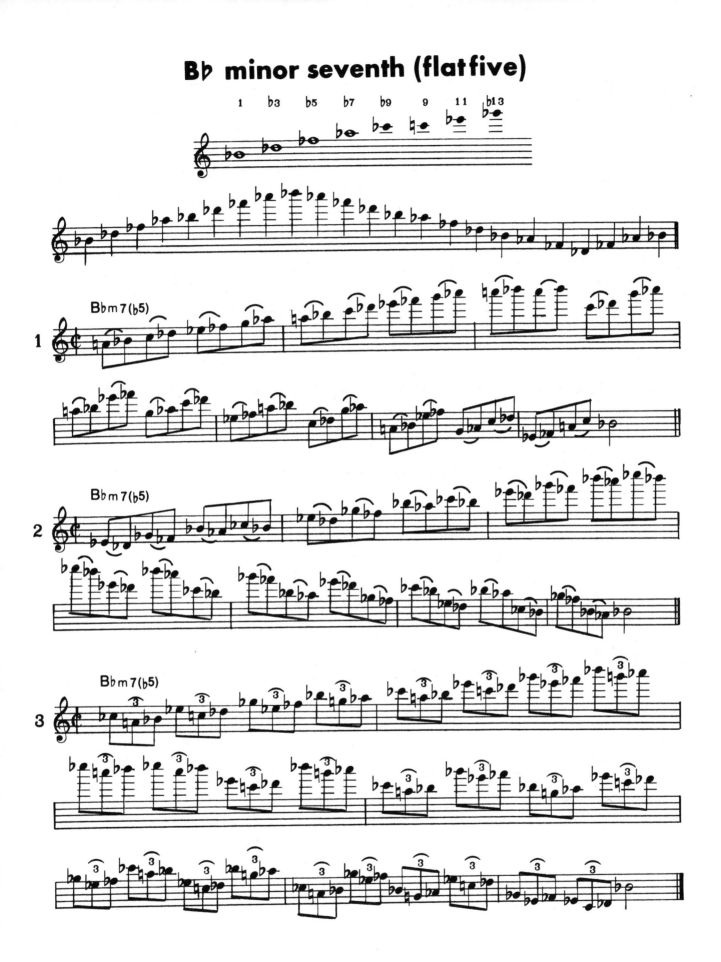

B♭ diminished seventh

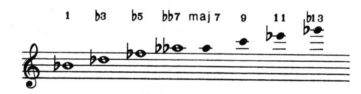

D major

38

D minor

D seventh

D minor seventh

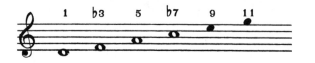

D minor seventh (flat five)

Dm7(b5)

Dm7(b5)

D diminished seventh

D°7

E♭ major

4

5

E♭ minor

1   ♭3   5   maj 7   9   13(6)

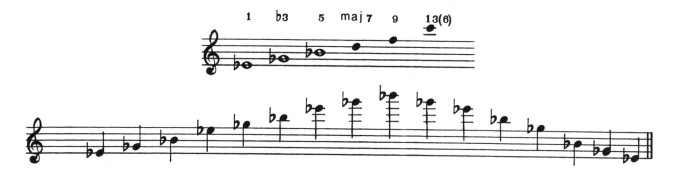

1   E♭m

E♭ seventh

E♭ minor seventh

Eb minor seventh (flat five)

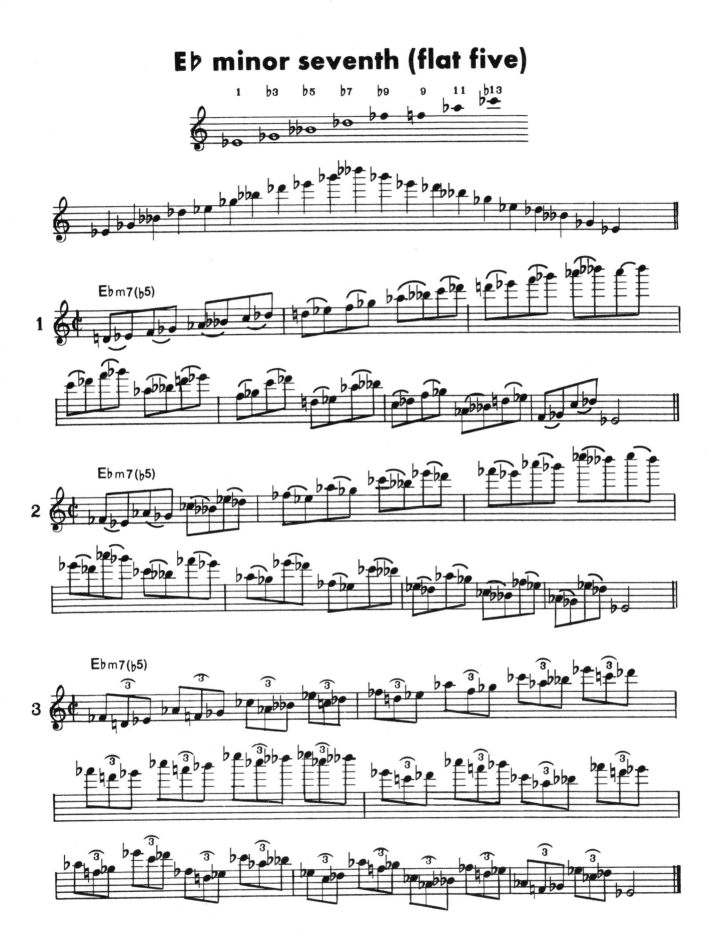

E♭ diminished seventh

A major

A minor

A seventh

4 A7

5 A7

A minor seventh

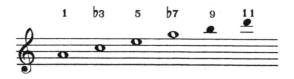

|1|♭3|5|♭7|9|11|

1 Am7

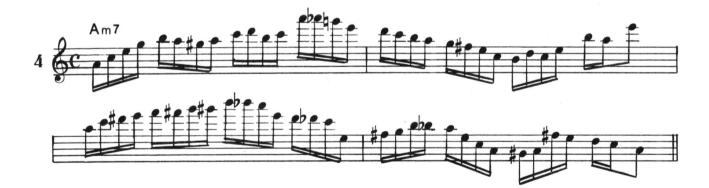

A minor seventh (flat five)

4 Am7(b5)

5 Am7(b5)

A diminished seventh

1   b3   b5   bb7   maj7   9   11   b13

1 A°7

2

3

4

5

A♭ major

1

2

3

A♭ minor

Ab seventh

A♭ minor seventh

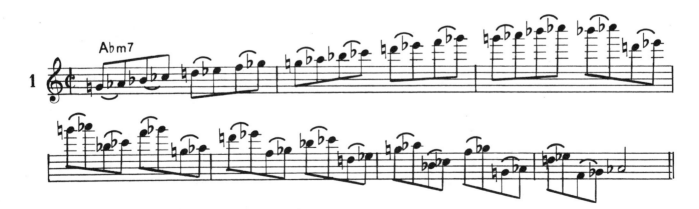

A♭ minor seventh (flat five)

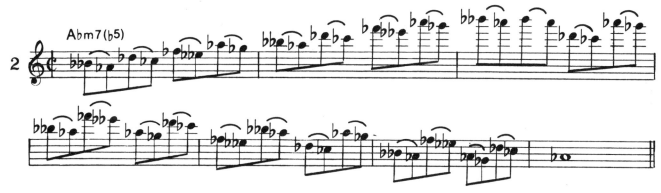

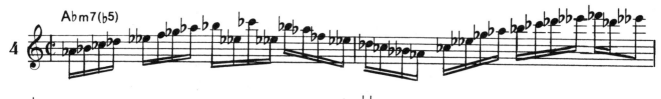

A♭ diminished seventh

2

3

4

5

E major

1

2

3

E minor

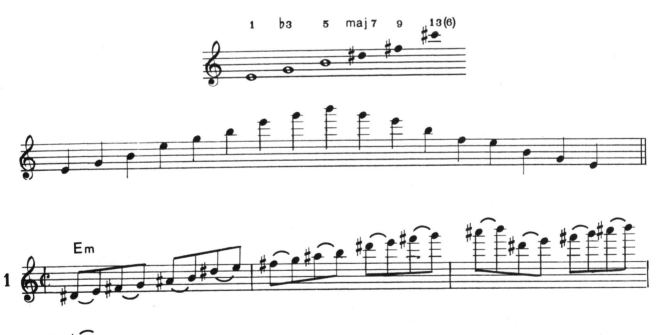

E seventh

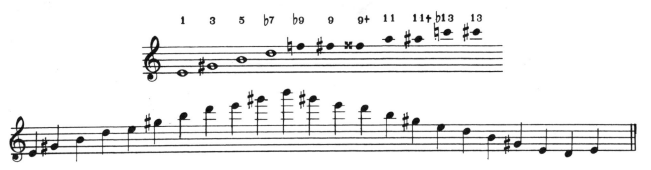

E minor seventh

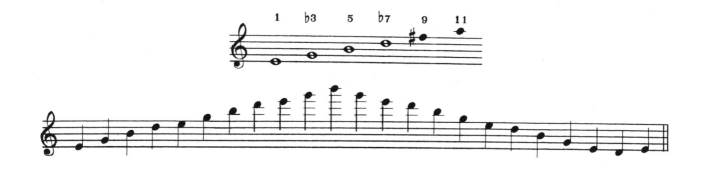

E minor seventh (flat five)

Em7(b5)

Em7(b5)

E diminished seventh

E°7

2

3

4

5

D♭ major

Db minor

D♭ seventh

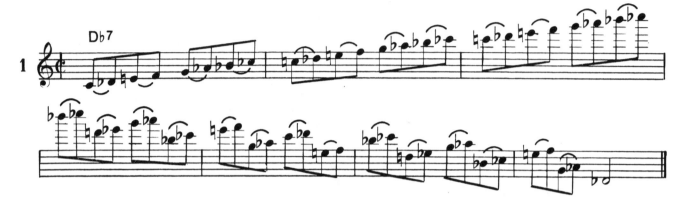

4

5

D♭ minor seventh

1

88

D♭ minor seventh (flat five)

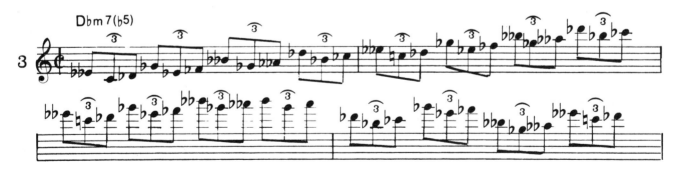

4

D♭m7(♭5)

5

D♭m7(♭5)

Db diminished seventh

| 1 | ♭3 | ♭5 | ♭♭7 | maj7 | 9 | 11 | ♭13 |

1

D♭°7

B major

B minor

B seventh

95

B minor seventh

B minor seventh (flat five)

4 Bm7(b5)

5 Bm7(b5)

B diminished seventh

1 B°7

2

3

4

5

G♭ major

G♭ minor

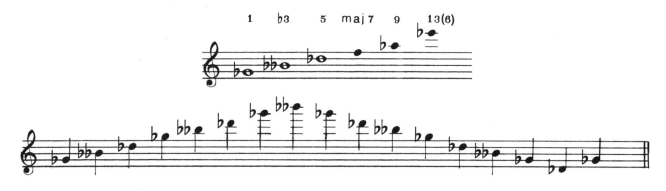

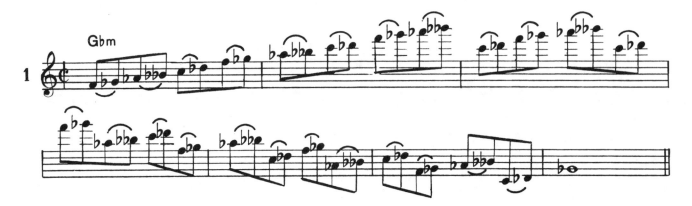

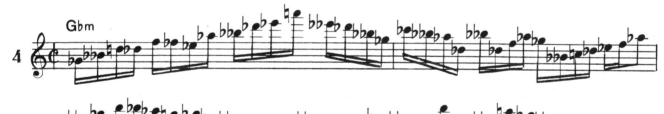

G♭ seventh

1

2

3

104

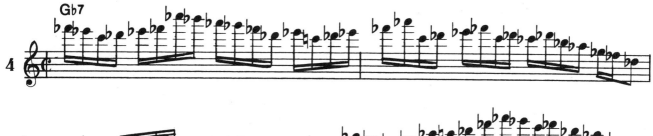

Gb minor seventh

G♭ minor seventh (flat five)

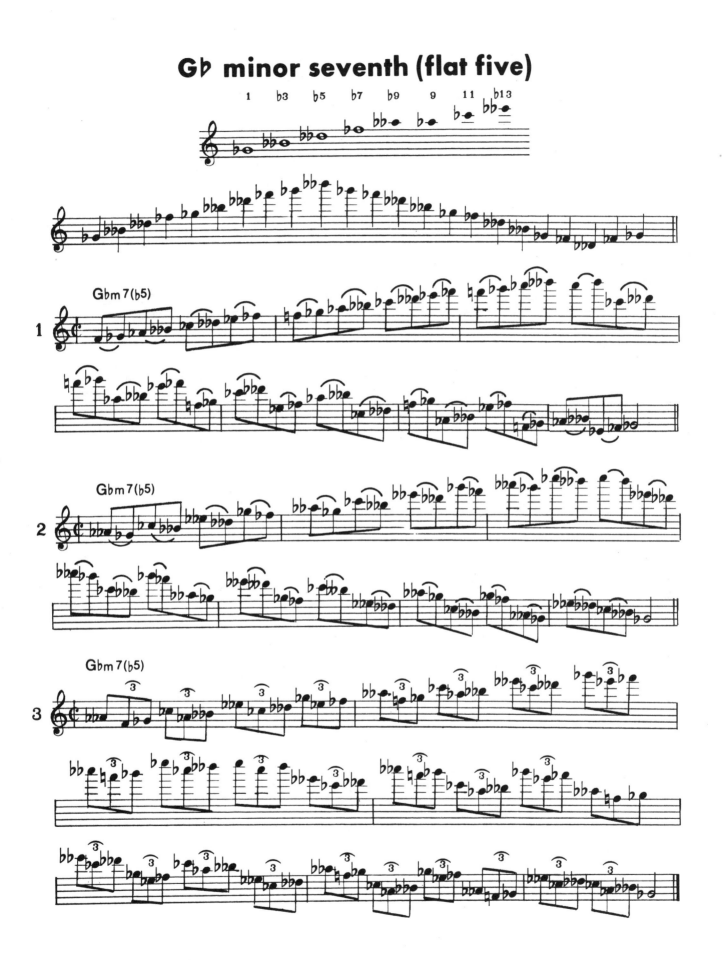

Gb diminished seventh

F# major

1

2

3

110

4

5

F# minor

1

F# seventh

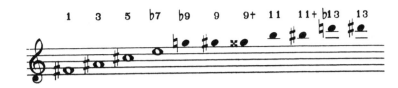

1

2

3

4 F#7

5 F#7

F# minor seventh

1 F#m7

F# minor seventh (flat five)

4 F#m7(b5)

5 F#m7(b5)

F# diminished seventh

| 1 | b3 | b5 | bb7 | maj 7 | 9 | 11 | b13 |

1 F#°7

2

3

4

5

C♭ major

119

Cb minor

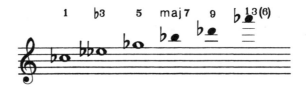

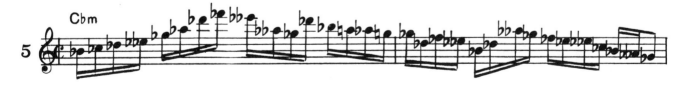

C♭ seventh

1

2

3

4

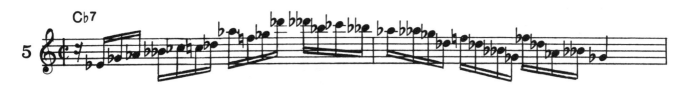

5

C♭ minor seventh

1

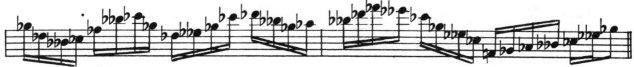

C♭ minor seventh (flat five)

125

Cb diminished seventh

126

C# major

C# minor

C# seventh

C# minor seventh

C# minor seventh (flat five)

134

C# diminished seventh

2

3

4

5

SUMMARY

Play all exercises 8va the 2nd time through.

Bb   Bbm   Bb7

Bbm7   Bbm7(b5)

Bb°

D   Dm   D7

Dm7   Dm7(b5)

D°

Eb   Ebm   Eb7

Ebm7   Ebm7(b5)

Eb°

138

A

Am

A7

Am7

Am7(b5)

A°

Ab

Abm

Ab7

Abm7

Abm7(b5)

Ab°

E

Em

E7

Em7

Em7(b5)

E°

Db

Dbm7

Db°

B

Bm7

B°

Gb

Gbm7

Gb°

F#

F#m7 ... F#m7(b5)

F#°

Cb ... Cbm ... Cb7

Cbm7 ... Cbm7(b5)

Cb°

C# ... C#m ... C#7

C#m7 ... C#m7(b5)

C#°

SECTION II

Studies

on

Chord Sequences

SECTION II
Studies on Chord Sequences

143

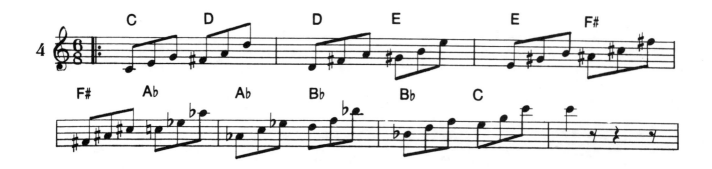

144

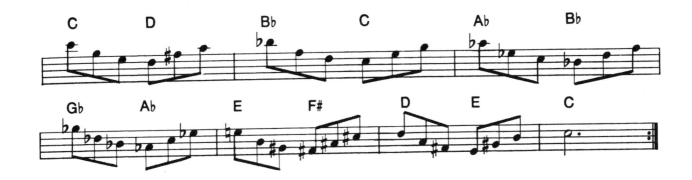

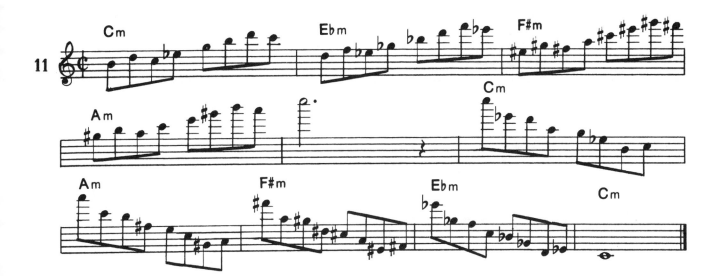

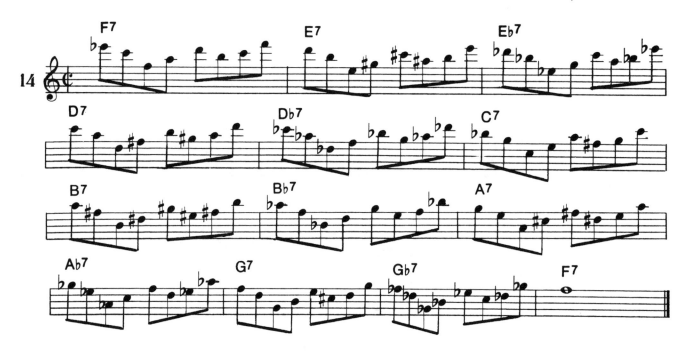

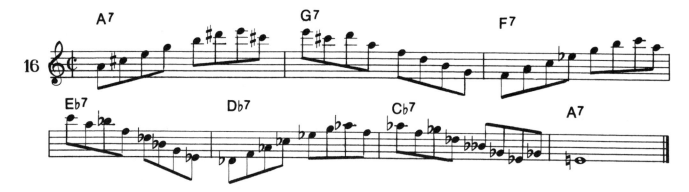

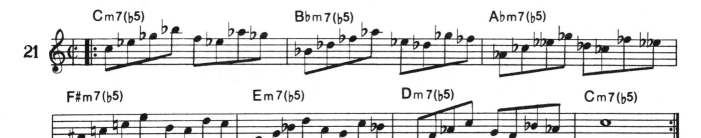

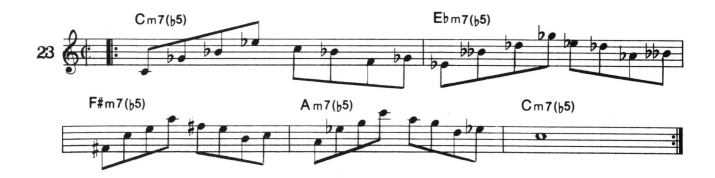

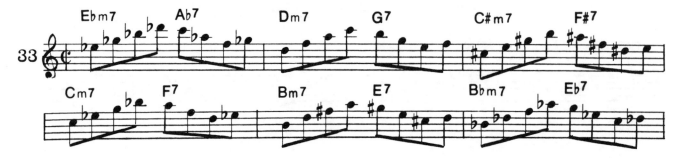

153

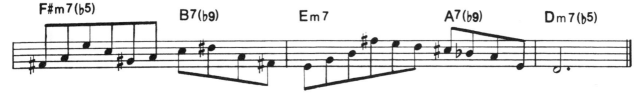

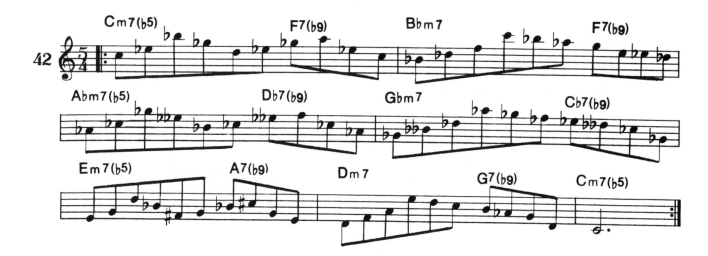

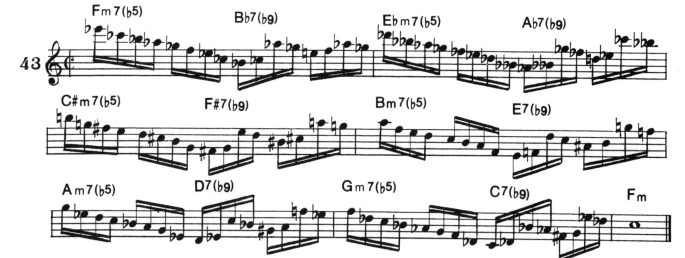

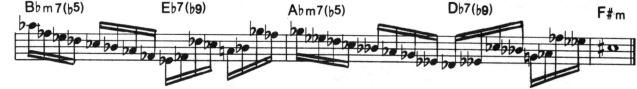

E   D#m7   C#m7   B

D   C#m7   Bm7   A

C   Bm7   Am7   G

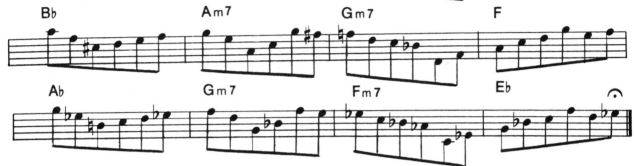

Bb   Am7   Gm7   F

Ab   Gm7   Fm7   Eb

F   Em7   Dm7   C

46

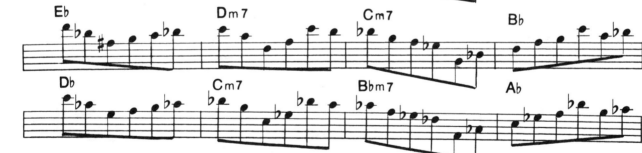

Eb   Dm7   Cm7   Bb

Db   Cm7   Bbm7   Ab

Cb   Bbm7   Abm7   Gb

A   G#m7   F#m7   E

G   F#m7   Em7   D

157

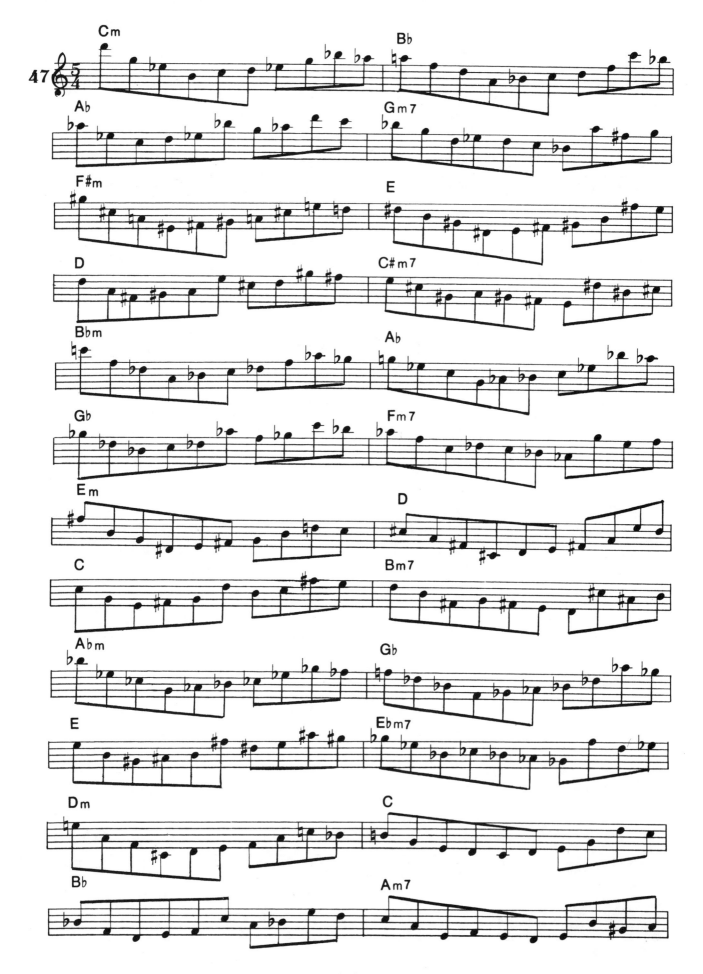

159

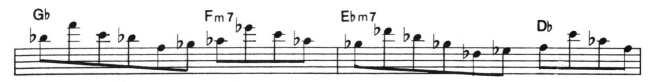